SCARY ADVENTURES AROUND THE WORLD

DO YOU DARE VISIT THE DEAD SEA?

BY MEGAN QUICK

Enslow
PUBLISHING

Please visit our website, www.enslow.com. For a free color catalog of all our high-quality books, call toll free 1-800-398-2504 or fax 1-877-980-4454.

Library of Congress Cataloging-in-Publication Data
Names: Quick, Megan, author.
Title: Do you dare visit the Dead Sea? / Megan Quick.
Description: Buffalo, New York : Enslow Publishing, [2024] | Series: Scary adventures around the world | Includes bibliographical references and index.
Identifiers: LCCN 2023003400 | ISBN 9781978536036 (library binding) | ISBN 9781978536029 (paperback) | ISBN 9781978536043 (ebook)
Subjects: LCSH: Dead Sea (Israel and Jordan)–Juvenile literature.
Classification: LCC DS110.D38 Q54 2024 | DDC 915.69404–dc23/eng/20230126
LC record available at https://lccn.loc.gov/2023003400

Published in 2024 by
Enslow Publishing
2544 Clinton Street
Buffalo, NY 14224

Portions of this work were originally authored by Therese Shea and published as *The Dead Sea*. All new material in this edition was authored by Megan Quick.

Designer: Tanya Dellaccio Keeney
Editor: Megan Quick

Photo credits: Series background Le Chernina/Shutterstock.com; cover, p. 1 Fadi Sultaneh/Shutterstock.com; pp. 5, 21 vvita/Shutterstock.com; p. 7 (bottom) irisphoto1/Shutterstock.com; p. 7 (top) cash1994/Shutterstock.com; p. 9 Suprun Vitaly/Shutterstock.com; p. 11 (bottom) M101Studio/Shutterstock.com; p. 11 (top) RuslanKphoto/Shutterstock.com; p. 13 RuslanDashinsky/iStock.com; p. 15 StockStudio Aerials/Shutterstock.com; p. 17 Sargey Boyko/Shutterstock.com; p. 19 (bottom) Bakusova/Shutterstock.com; p. 19 (top) Sean Pavone/Shutterstock.com.

Printed in the United States of America

CPSIA compliance information: Batch #CSENS24: For further information contact Enslow Publishing at 1-800-398-2504.

Find us on

CONTENTS

Words in the glossary appear in **bold** type the first time they are used in the text.

A STRANGE SEA

Have you ever been to a lake? You may have seen animals like fish or frogs, as well as plenty of plants. Most lakes are full of life—but not the Dead Sea! That's right. The Dead Sea is a lake, not a sea. And like the name sounds, there is not much life there.

You might not want to go for a swim in a place called the Dead Sea. Its name sounds pretty scary. But before you decide, let's find out more about this very unusual body of water.

FIND THE FACTS

TODAY THE DEAD SEA IS SURROUNDED BY LAND. BUT MILLIONS OF YEARS AGO, IT WAS PART OF THE MEDITERRANEAN SEA. HUGE PIECES OF THE EARTH'S SURFACE SHIFTED OVER TIME UNTIL THE BODY OF WATER BECAME LANDLOCKED.

The Dead Sea is located in the Judean Desert.

WHERE IN THE WORLD?

The Dead Sea lies between the countries of Israel and Jordan. The West Bank also borders its northwestern shores. The Jordan River flows into the lake from the north. The lake gets almost all of its water from this river.

The Dead Sea is the lowest body of water in the world. It is also the lowest point on Earth's surface. The lake is about 1,427 feet (435 m) below sea level. The shores of the Dead Sea are the lowest dry point on Earth.

FIND THE FACTS

THE AREA AROUND THE DEAD SEA IS A DESERT. IT GETS VERY HOT AND ONLY RECEIVES ABOUT 2.5 INCHES (64 MM) OF RAIN PER YEAR.

LEBANON

SYRIA

MEDITERRANEAN SEA

WEST
BANK

JORDAN RIVER

DEAD SEA

ISRAEL

JORDAN

EGYPT

The Dead Sea is in
a part of the world
called the Middle East.

SUPER SALINE

The Dead Sea has a fitting name. There is almost no life in its waters. The lake is not dangerous for humans and land animals, but fish, plants, and other **aquatic** animals cannot **survive** there. This is because the Dead Sea is very different from other bodies of water.

The Dead Sea is very salty. It is much saltier than any ocean water. It contains between 28 and 35 percent **saline**. Is that a lot? It is 10 times saltier than the ocean!

FIND THE FACTS

THE DEAD SEA IS ALSO KNOWN AS THE SALT SEA.

SPECIAL SALT

The Dead Sea is one of the saltiest bodies of water in the world. The reason for its high salt level is **evaporation**. In summer, the area has reached nearly 122°F (49.9°C). The heat causes water flowing into the Dead Sea to evaporate quickly. The salt in the water gets left behind.

The salt in the Dead Sea is not the kind you find in your kitchen. There are 35 kinds of **mineral** salts in the lake. These include calcium, iodine, and magnesium.

FIND THE FACTS

MANY PEOPLE VISIT THE DEAD SEA TO FEEL BETTER. THE MINERALS IN THE WATER AND MUD MAY HELP SKIN PROBLEMS AS WELL AS OTHER PARTS OF THE BODY.

It's okay to get dirty in the Dead Sea! The mud is good for your skin.

SIGNS OF LIFE

You won't see fish swimming in the Dead Sea, but there is some life there. Scientists have found tiny life forms called **bacteria** in craters at the bottom of the lake. They are able to live there because fresh water is leaking into the lake from underground springs.

Studying life at the bottom of the Dead Sea is not easy. Divers must weigh themselves down so the salty water doesn't push them up. And they must wear special masks so the salty water won't burn their eyes.

FIND THE FACTS

IF YOU GO FOR A SWIM IN THE DEAD SEA, KEEP YOUR HEAD ABOVE THE WATER! IF YOU HAPPEN TO GET A MOUTHFUL OF WATER, THE HIGH LEVEL OF SALT WILL CHOKE YOU AND MAKE IT HARD TO BREATHE.

THE DYING DEAD SEA

The Dead Sea is about 31 miles (50 km) long and 9 miles (15 km) across at its widest point. But it is getting smaller every year. The Dead Sea is slowly drying up. People's use of the Jordan River is a major reason for this change.

Governments and other groups are using the water from the Jordan River before it can reach the Dead Sea. They use it for businesses, farms, and drinking water. Meanwhile, the water in the Dead Sea keeps evaporating, with little water coming to replace it.

SINKHOLE

Much of the land seen here was once covered by the waters of the Dead Sea.

FIND THE FACTS

AS THE DEAD SEA WATERS PULL BACK, SINKHOLES ARE FORMING ALONG THE EDGES OF THE LAKE. THERE WERE MORE THAN 7,000 SINKHOLES IN 2022. PEOPLE HAVE BEEN HURT FALLING INTO THESE HOLES.

CAN IT BE SAVED?

The Dead Sea doesn't contain many living things. But the area around it is full of life. Birds make their nests near the water. Land animals live near the shore. And as the Dead Sea gets smaller, the animals and their homes are in danger.

Saving the Dead Sea is not easy. A major plan to run a pipeline from the Red Sea to the Dead Sea was **abandoned** in 2021. Groups are still trying to figure out how to fill up the salt lake. It will be expensive and countries will need to work together.

FIND THE FACTS

THE WATER LEVEL OF THE DEAD SEA DROPS ABOUT 3.6 FEET (1.1 M) EVERY YEAR. SCIENTISTS SAY THE DEAD SEA WILL NOT DISAPPEAR COMPLETELY, BUT IT COULD BECOME A SMALL LAKE.

Ibexes are wild goats that are found near the shores of the Dead Sea.

PAGES FROM THE PAST

Imagine finding papers written thousands of years ago. This is what happened from 1947 to 1956 in caves by the Dead Sea! Over 900 **scrolls** were found dating between 250 BCE and 68 CE. The scrolls are not on paper like we use today. They are made of animal skin and **papyrus**. The scrolls contain prayers, songs, and other texts.

No one is sure who wrote the Dead Sea Scrolls, but they're some of the oldest religious writings ever found. They have helped people learn more about the Jewish and Christian religions.

Some of the Dead Sea Scrolls were found in these caves.

FIND THE FACTS

MOST OF THE DEAD SEA SCROLLS WERE NOT IN ONE PIECE WHEN THEY WERE DISCOVERED. THE PIECES HAD TO BE CAREFULLY PUT BACK TOGETHER.

DO YOU DARE?

Now that you know more about the Dead Sea, do you dare visit? In spite of the name, it is not a scary spot! People come from all over to float in the salty water, enjoy the healthy minerals, and learn more about the area's ancient history.

The Dead Sea is a place that is not like anywhere else in the world. It is also in danger of losing much of its water. People will need to work together to save this unusual area before it is too late.

FIND THE FACTS

VISITORS ARE LESS LIKELY TO GET A SUNBURN AT THE DEAD SEA. ITS LOCATION WELL BELOW SEA LEVEL MEANS THE SUN'S RAYS ARE NOT AS STRONG. BUT DON'T SKIP THE SUNBLOCK! BURNS CAN STILL HAPPEN.

Here, the sun rises over the Dead Sea.

GLOSSARY

abandon: To leave behind.

aquatic: Having to do with water.

bacteria: Tiny creatures that can only be seen with a microscope.

evaporation: The change from a liquid to a gas.

landlocked: Surrounded by land on all sides.

mineral: Matter important in small amounts for the health of animals.

papyrus: Writing material made from the papyrus plant and used by ancient peoples.

saline: Having to do with containing salt.

scroll: A roll of paper or other matter for writing a document.

sinkhole: A hole in the ground that forms when rocks or soil are removed by flowing water.

survive: To live through something.

FOR MORE INFORMATION

Books

Doeden, Matt. *Travel to Israel*. Minneapolis, MN: Lerner, 2022.

Jackson, Tom. *Wonders of the World*. New York, NY: DK, 2022.

Websites

DeadSea.com
DeadSea.com
Find out everything you need to know to plan your trip to the Dead Sea.

Kiddle: The Dead Sea Scrolls
kids.kiddle.co/Dead_Sea_scrolls
Check out images and cool facts about the Dead Sea Scrolls.

INDEX